JANE AUSTEN'S PRAYERS

COMFORTING WORDS FROM A MOST BELOVED AUTHOR

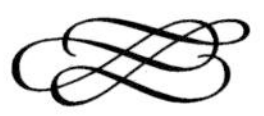

EMMA DARLINGTON

Jane Austen's Prayers

EMMA DARLINGTON

Jane Austen's Prayers: Comforting Words From A Most Beloved Author
Introduced by Emma Darlington

A catalogue record of this book is available from the British Library.

ISBN 978-18382811-0-6

Published by Brite Bird Press
www.britebirdpress.com

Inside Image: From a watercolour by James Andrews of Maidenhead based on an unfinished work by Cassandra Austen. Engraving by William Home Lizars. A Memoir of Jane Austen by her nephew J. E. Austen-Leigh, Vicar of Bray, Berks. London: Richard Bentley, New Burlington Street, Publisher in Ordinary to her Majesty, 1870. Public Domain.

For my family, with love and prayers.

For all whom we love and value,
for every friend and connection,
we equally pray;
however divided and far asunder,
we know that we are alike before Thee,
and under Thine eye.

— JANE AUSTEN PRAYER

A whole family assembling regularly for the purpose of prayer is fine!

— FANNY PRICE, MANSFIELD PARK

JANE AUSTEN.

LONDON: RICHARD BENTLEY, 1870.

CONTENTS

INTRODUCTION

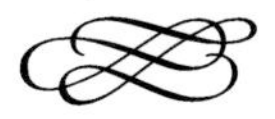

'*Prayers composed by my ever dear sister Jane*' is written on one of the two manuscripts containing the three prayers known to have been written by Jane Austen.

Jane's sister Cassandra treasured the prayers until her death in 1845. She bequeathed them to her niece Cassandra Esten Austen, the eldest daughter of their brother Charles. The manuscripts are believed to be in the handwriting of Jane, Cassandra and Henry their brother. They were placed in a Sotheby's sale in 1927 by Jane's great nieces, Jane and Emma Austen, along with a collection of Jane Austen papers which subsequently sold for £175.

They were acquired by William Matson Roth who was a California book collector from San Francisco. He brought them into print in 1940 using his own Colt Press in San Francisco. He produced 300 copies which were typed up in capital letters and printed on poor quality paper which he then distributed to book collectors.

In 1957, he donated the manuscripts to Mills College in Oakland, California. They are cared for by the F W. Olin Library where they remain to this day.

It is wonderful to think that these prayers are over 200 years old. On closer inspection, the prayers themselves are folded into leaves.

On the fold of the first leaf is written '*Prayers Composed by my ever dear Sister Jane*', and on the opposite side the first prayer is titled '*Evening Prayer*'. Penciled lightly under the title on the first page are the words '*Charles Austen*', who was Jane and Cassandra's 'own particular little brother'.

The second and third prayers are written on the second sheet of manuscript and start with '*Father of Heaven!*' and '*Almighty God!*'.

It is most likely that the prayers would be used for evening devotions, read aloud by one of the family followed by everyone reciting the Lord's Prayer.

As you read along with these beautiful, heartfelt prayers, remember that Jane embraced the Christian faith and was a deeply religious person. This does suggest that her novels were written with more religious feeling than we might have thought.

Jane's followers will have read and reread her novels many times, and she is well known as the author of *Pride and Prejudice, Emma, Sense and Sensibility, Mansfield Park, Northanger Abbey,* and *Persuasion.* Many television series and films have increased Jane's fame, and as new readers come along, her popularity continues to grow.

There will be many followers of Jane's who are unaware she wrote these prayers, and will be reading them for the first time.

Jane steered clear of any sort of preaching in her novels, although she does cover church topics and writes about characterful clergymen. Her grandfather, father, two brothers, numerous cousins and distant relations were all clergymen, so she was surrounded by the church and their leaders. It was a topic she knew a lot about and could comfortably write about.

She avoided religious matters in her private letters with her family, and any reference to church in her surviving letters was to talk about the weather, or the delivery of a particular sermon. Being a good Christian was a way of life for Jane, so there was no need to discuss it in any detail.

One prayer passage reads, '*May we now, and on each return of night, consider how the past day has been spent by us, what have been our prevailing Thoughts, Words, and Actions during it.*'

Jane strongly held the Christian belief that what a person did each day was more important than what a person said, and this is reflected in her prayers.

They are written in a similar style to those found in the 1662 *Book of Common Prayer* which she would have known by heart. Jane asks God for forgiveness, protection, health and safety for her family and friends, and offers her thanks for the blessings she has received from Him.

Jane may have copied them out to take with her when visiting friends or family as they are folded very neatly, or for taking out for easy reading by candlelight. Whatever the reason, they are beautifully written, and give us a glimpse into her heart.

CHRONOLOGY

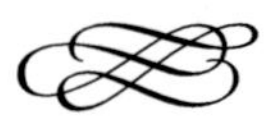

JANE AUSTEN: 16 December 1775 - 18 July 1817

1764
26 April, Reverend George Austen married Miss Cassandra Leigh at Walcot Church, Bath. The couple move to Deane Rectory and their first three children are born here, James, George and Edward.

1765
Mr and Mrs Hancock (George Austen's sister) and their daughter Eliza (Betsy) return from India.

1768
The Austen family move to Steventon Rectory and this is where five more children join the family, Henry, Cassandra, Francis, Jane, and Charles.

1773
Cassandra Elizabeth Austen is born on 9 January at Steventon.

1775
Jane Austen is born on 16 December at Steventon.

1776
In the Spring, Jane is formally received into St Nicholas Church, Steventon as it is written in the Steventon Church Register.

1781
Jane's cousin Eliza Hancock marries Jean-François Capot de Feuillide in France.

1782
Amateur theatricals take place at Steventon.

1783
Edward Austen is adopted by Mr and Mrs Thomas Knight of Godmersham, Kent.
Jane, Cassandra and their cousin Jane go to school, first at Oxford and then Southampton. Jane falls ill of typhus fever and almost dies.

1785
Jane, Cassandra and their cousin Jane spend two years at the Abbey House School, Reading.

1787
Between now and 1793, Jane is writing her *Juvenilia*, sketches, plays and stories collecting them into three manuscript notebooks titled, *Volume the First, Volume the Second* and *Volume the Third*.
It is around this time that Jane writes the mock entries in the Steventon Church Register.

1792
Cassandra is engaged to Reverend Tom Fowle, one of her father's pupils.

1793
Jane is 17 years old when her first two fondest nieces are born.
Edward Austen's first child Frances (Fanny) Catherine is born at Rowling, Kent, on 23 January.
James Austen's first child (Jane) Anna is born at Deane, Hampshire, on 15 April.
Jane writes the last piece of her *Juvenilia*.

1794
Jane was confirmed into the Anglican Church. She is given a prayer book and writes her name and the date 23 April 1794 inside.

1795
Jane writes *Elinor and Marianne*, an early version of *Sense and Sensibility*.
3 May, James's wife Anne dies and their daughter Anna is sent to live at Steventon Rectory for months at a time.
Tom Lefroy visits Ashe Rectory for Christmas and has a flirtation with Jane.

1796
The first preserved letters written by Jane date from this year. Jane starts writing *First Impressions*, which later becomes *Pride and Prejudice* after a visit to her brother Edward at Godmersham, Kent.

1797
Cassandra's fiancée Reverend Tom Fowle dies of fever at San Domingo and is buried at sea.
In November, Mr Austen offers *First Impressions* to Thomas Cadell who rejects it 'sight unseen'.
Henry Austen marries Jane's cousin Eliza de Feuillide in London on 31 December.

1798
Jane starts writing her novel *Susan*, published as *Northanger Abbey* after her death.
17 November, James Austen's first son (James) Edward is born at Deane, Hampshire. He was Jane's fondest nephew and wrote her *Memoirs*.

1799
Jane spends May and June in Bath with her brother Edward, his wife Elizabeth and two of their children. They stay at a house in Queen Square.

1800
In December, Jane's father George Austen announces his retirement and the move to Bath. It is said that when Jane was told the news, she fainted away.

1801
In May, the Austen family leave Steventon and settle in Bath. A lease is taken on 4 Sydney Place from September, and the family visit Devon whilst the house is being redecorated.

1802
Jane receives a proposal of marriage from Harris Bigg Wither of Manydown which she initially accepts and later declines.
Jane revises *Susan (Northanger Abbey)*.

1803
Jane sells *Susan* (later titled *Northanger Abbey)* to Crosby for £10.
In November the family visit Lyme Regis in Dorset.

1804
Jane is writing *The Watsons* which is never finished.
The family lease a house in Green Park Gardens, Bath, and once again visit Lyme Regis.
Madam Lefroy of Ashe is killed in a riding accident on Jane's birthday, 16 December.

1805
George Austen dies on 21 January and is buried at St Swithin's Walcot Church, Bath.
James Austen's daughter Caroline is born on 18 June.

1806
Jane, her mother and sister leave Bath for good.
In July they visit Mrs Austen's relatives at Stoneleigh in Warwickshire and Adlestrop, Gloucestershire.
The Austen ladies and Martha Lloyd move to Southampton to live with Jane's brother Frank and his new wife Mary.

1807
Edward Austen arranges a large family gathering at Chawton Great House.

1808
10 October, Edward Austen's wife Elizabeth dies at Godmersham, shortly after the birth of their eleventh child.

1809
7 July the Austen ladies and Martha Lloyd move to Chawton Cottage, Hampshire.
Jane writes the famous MAD letter to Crosby to try and get her novel *Susan* published.

1810
Sense and Sensibility accepted for publication by Thomas Egerton.

1811
Jane is writing *Mansfield Park* in February.
Sense and Sensibility is published on 30 October 'By A Lady'.
Jane visits Henry and Eliza in London.
Jane starts revising *First Impressions* into *Pride and Prejudice* through the Winter months.

1813
Pride and Prejudice is published 28 January.
In April, Jane goes to London to nurse her cousin Eliza de Feuillide who is ill. She dies on 25 April.
Jane finishes *Mansfield Par*k in July, and it is accepted for publication by Egerton.

1814
Jane starts writing *Emma* in January.
Mansfield Park is published 9 May and sold out by the autumn.

1815
Jane starts writing *Persuasion* in August.
Henry falls seriously ill and Jane stays in London to nurse him.
Emma is finished and Jane visits the Prince Regent's Library at Carlton House. Jane receives a request to dedicate it to the Prince Regent, and it is published in December by John Murray (title page dated 1816).

1816
Jane is now 40 years old and once her health begins to fail, she visits Cheltenham in the Spring seeking a cure.
Jane finishes *Persuasion* in July, and rewrites the ending. Henry buys back *Susan* from the publisher which Jane revises as *Catherine*. He later changes the title to *Northanger Abbey*.

1817
Jane starts writing *Sanditon* 27 January and on 18 March has to leave it unfinished.
Jane's nieces visit their ill Aunt Jane at Chawton Cottage as remembered in their *Memoirs*.
24 May, Cassandra takes Jane to Winchester for medical treatment and they lodge at 8 College Street.
18 July Jane dies the arms of her sister Cassandra.
24 July the funeral takes place and Jane is buried in Winchester Cathedral.

1818
Northanger Abbey and *Persuasion* are bound and published posthumously by John Murray. Jane's brother Henry includes a *Biographical Notice of the Author* as a short prefix.

1845
Cassandra Austen dies and Jane's possessions are divided.

1870
Jane's fondest nephew, J. Edward Austen Leigh publishes *A Memoir of Jane Austen.*

1884
Lord Brabourne, the eldest son of Jane's niece Fanny, publishes the first edition of *Letters of Jane Austen.*

1927
Jane's *Prayers* are placed in a Sotheby's sale by her great nieces, Jane and Emma, descendants of her brother Charles.

1957
William Matson Roth gifts the *Prayers* to F. W. Olin Library, Mills College, Oakland, California where they remain to this day.

THE NOVELS

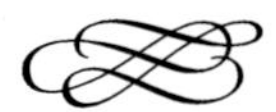

Jane Austen has a wonderful skill in revealing animated characters to her readers. She has brought us many clergymen, young beautiful women, rich prospective husbands, and tales of love, money, and ultimately happiness.

There has been much speculation about who and what inspired her writing, especially as she lived most of her life in the countryside. It was a life full towns and villages, large families and friends, where people all knew each other and seemed to be interlinked somehow through marriage or relations.

As the daughter of a clergyman, Jane would help her father with his Church duties, and was familiar with the trials of everyday life from an early age. Jane had many childhood friends, cousins, and relations, whose personalities and life events we can speculate she wrote about in each of her novels.

Kent gave Jane new characters to draw on, as Edward had been adopted by a rich family and Kent was a world away from the rural villages of Hampshire. She was invited to attend many dinners and dances, and spent time in London staying with Henry whilst she polished and negotiated her works. Through her Navy brothers, she had a good grasp of the war, politics and international events.

Four of Jane's novels were published in her lifetime, and two after her death. *The Watsons* was left unfinished, and Jane had to put *Sanditon* to one side when she became too ill to write.

In 1817, Jane estimated that she had earned around £600 in pewter from her novels. This was broken down into £140 for the first edition of *Sense and Sensibility*, £110 for the copyright of *Pride and Prejudice,* and £350 for the first edition of *Mansfield Park* and the second edition of *Sense and Sensibility*.

PUBLISHED NOVELS

SENSE AND SENSIBILITY

Drafted as *Elinor and Marianne* around 1795, *Sense and Sensibility* is about the close relationship between two sisters, one with practical good sense and the other sensitive and emotional.

Mrs Dashwood is driven away from Norland, her family home, after the death of her husband. The estate is inherited by a son from a previous marriage, John Dashwood. His wife Fanny persuades John to break his promise to his dying father leaving the Dashwood ladies with little money to live on. A move brings a circle of eligible men for the two sisters including Fanny's brother Edward, the dashing villain Willoughby, and the steady Colonel Brandon.

Sense and Sensibility was originally written in letter form, although Jane later changed it to direct narrative as the sisters were never apart.

It was published in 1811, and sold so well a second edition came out in 1813. Jane was still receiving royalties from the novel in March 1817.

PRIDE AND PREJUDICE

Jane started writing *First Impressions* in October 1796 and finished it around August of the following year. She was then 21 years old. The Austen family enjoyed it so much, that in November 1797 Jane's father offered it to a publisher in London who declined it 'sight unseen'.

Fourteen years later in 1811, Jane began revising it and it was 'lop't and crop't' and finally published by Thomas Egerton on 28 January 1813. Jane called it *'my own darling Child'* in a letter to Cassandra. Jane was not publicly known as the author as it was simply titled 'By the Author of "*Sense and Sensibility*".'

Pride and Prejudice is a romantic novel with Elizabeth and Jane Bennet at its heart. They are two of five sisters, who have no inheritance to speak of so must marry well. Mr Bingley is a rich bachelor and the new tenant of Netherfield, who along with his friend Mr Darcy causes all kinds of excitement for the local residents. Mr Collins, a cousin and pompous clergyman has his own marriage proposal in mind, and a rogue Mr Wickham threatens the Bennet family name which could mean the end of happiness for all the sisters.

Pride and Prejudice sold so well, a second edition was printed the same autumn and a third in 1817. The reading public adored Elizabeth, and it is still Jane's most popular novel having sold over 20 million copies worldwide.

MANSFIELD PARK

Mansfield Park was written in full at Chawton in 1811 and published in 1814.

The heroine of the novel is Fanny Price who at ten years old is sent away to live with relatives at Mansfield Park. Fanny misses her family terribly, especially her brother William, and is comforted by her cousin Edward. Mrs Bertram and her pug spend most of the novel on the sofa surrounded by her spoilt children and her wicked sister Mrs Norris, who treats Fanny like a servant.

Enter Henry and Mary Crawford who arrive from London to shake up the household. As the children rehearse the play *Lovers Vows*, the story gathers momentum until Sir Thomas returns and puts everything in its place.

Some speculate that the story was inspired by Jane's brother Edward who was adopted when Jane was a young girl. He moved to Kent which is miles away from the family home, and they must have missed him terribly.

As a novel, it was not as well received as *Pride and Prejudice* and there were mixed reviews. Fanny was either thought delightful or very dull. It seemed to lack the lightness of her other novels.

It sold well enough for a second edition in 1816. The naval references in the novel came from tales reported back from Jane's brothers Charles and Frank, and Jane writes in the novel that Fanny receives a topaz cross from her brother William, just as Jane and Cassandra did from their brother Charles.

EMMA

After the sweetness of *Pride and Prejudice,* Jane had decided to write about a less perfect character. Before she began the novel, she told Cassandra, *'I am going to take a heroine whom no one but myself will much like.'*

The opening line of the novel reads, '*Emma Woodhouse, handsome, clever, and rich, with a comfortable home and happy disposition seemed to unite some of the best blessings of existence and had lived nearly twenty-one years in the world with very little to distress or vex her.*'

Emma lives with her father at Hartfield in Highbury, a small village where everyone knows everyone, and Emma is bored. Her governess has recently married, and Emma believes she has made their match. She then interferes with the love lives of her friends causing a tangle of misunderstandings, witnessed by Mr Knightly who is the lone member of Emma's circle who will disagree with her and chastise her manners. Emma grows and matures throughout the novel, and is shown how to improve her own character through love.

Jane referred to her novels as her children, writing to her niece Anna, whose new daughter she had not yet seen, *'As I wish very much to see your Jemima, I am sure you will like to see my Emma.'*

Written in 1814, *Emma* was ready in March 1815. Egerton delayed publishing whilst he negotiated with Murray, another successful publisher. They eventually agreed that Jane would publish at her own expense with Murray receiving 10% of the profits. The *Morning Chronicle* announced the publication of *Emma* on 23 December 1815. This was the last novel Jane published in her lifetime.

Jane reluctantly dedicated *Emma* to the Prince Regent who was known to gamble and have mistresses. She sent a dedicated and specially bound copy to the future King that is now in the Royal Household and on display at the Royal Pavilion.

NORTHANGER ABBEY

Drafted in 1798, *Susan* is a gothic novel which was a popular genre at the time it was written. It was sold to Crosby in 1803 for £10 who decided not to publish. Jane wrote to the publisher six years later to ask for its return, and in 1816 was able to buy it back for £10. She then '*Put it on the Shelve for the present.*'

Jane had to change the heroine's name to Catherine as another novel titled *Susan* had been published in 1809.

Northanger Abbey is about Catherine Moreland, one of ten daughters, who lives a sheltered life in the country. She is taken to Bath as a young girl by Mr and Mrs Allen to essentially 'come out' after Mr Allen is ordered to Bath for his health. She is influenced by Henry Tilney, Mrs Thorpe, and Isabella who is engaged to her brother, and the villain of the novel John Thorpe. Catherine becomes engrossed in *The Mysteries of Udolpho,* and a visit to *Northanger Abbey* fuels her imagination further as she discovers the people around her in pursuit of her own happiness.

Northanger Abbey was published posthumously together with *Persuasion* in 1818.

PERSUASION

Written in 1815, it was the last novel Jane was to complete. *Persuasion* is a wartime love story about Frederick Wentworth and Anne Elliot who meet again after years apart. His low social status and lack of wealth made Anne's family view him as an unsuitable husband and no match for a woman of Kellynch Hall, the family estate. His marriage proposal was refused by Anne, and she later regrets this decision. When Captain Wentworth returns from sea he finds Anne's family on the brink of financial ruin, and his sister a tenant in Kellynch Hall. Can he forgive Anne for breaking his heart and find love elsewhere, or will they rekindle their love?

Some scenes are set in Bath, and the story includes a visit to Lyme Regis and the well known fall from The Cobb.

Jane finished the novel in July, although she was unhappy with the ending so rewrote it. It was published six months after her death by her brother Henry who chose the title. Jane's manuscript of *Persuasion* and the alternative ending remains intact, and is sometimes on display.

Both shorter than Jane's other novels, *Persuasion* and *Northanger Abbey* are bound in four volumes and sold as one publication. They were published on 20 December 1817, although the title page is dated 1818.

This is the first time Jane Austen is named as the author, although she never saw her name in print.

UNFINISHED NOVELS

THE WATSONS

Jane drafted 17,500 words of *The Watsons* around 1804. A large and unhappy family, the Watsons are forced to leave the parsonage when their father dies. Jane's own father died in 1805, and it is thought the sadness of the story meant it was never completed. The original manuscript is still in existence and was published in 1871.

SANDITON

Started on 24 January 1817, the 24,000 words of *Sanditon* were divided into 12 chapters. Jane set it aside due to illness on 18 March that same year. She had discussed the novel with her family and referred to it as *The Brothers,* who want to turn their fishing village into a spa town. The manuscript is intact, and was published in 1925 under the title *Fragment of a Novel.*

JANE AUSTEN AND HER FAITH

'*Prayers composed by my ever dear sister Jane*' is written on the fold of the prayers written by Jane, and treasured by her sister Cassandra until her death.

They are beautiful, and heartfelt, and remind us that Jane embraced the Christian faith and was a deeply religious person.

Jane was born at Steventon Rectory on 16 December 1775, and baptized by her father Reverend George Austen upon her birth.

It was a particular harsh winter, so it was the following Spring before Jane made her first trip along the leafy lane to be entered into the church. Her entry in the Steventon Church Register reads that she was accepted on 5 April 1776, which was in fact Good Friday.

Jane would have heard prayers as a child said over her cot as she slept, and later as she knelt at her bedside before bed. Her family often read the bible to her, with its many stories where good triumphs over evil, or where there is a reformation of some sort.

Cassandra was almost three when Jane was born, and they would be inseparable throughout their lives. There were already five brothers at home. James was ten, George was nine (and lived away), Edward was eight, Henry was four, and Frank was one and a half. Charles was to follow Jane four years later.

Jane was close to all her siblings, and their love for one another increased as they grew older. One of Jane's nieces said, '*The family talk had much of spirit and vivacity, and it was never troubled by disagreements as it was not their habit to argue with each other - There always was perfect harmony amongst the brothers and sisters.*'

At home, the family would sit and read in the evenings. James and Mrs Austen were known for writing poetry, and the family would read passages from novels, letters or plays. They would read the Bible and close the evening with one of the family reading prayers aloud, followed by everyone saying the Lord's Prayer.

In general, life at the rectory was busy with lots of people coming and going, with everyone expected to contribute.

Jane helped her father with his church duties, and would have been familiar with birth, sickness and death from an early age.

On Sundays, Jane probably stood next to her father as he gave God's blessing to the people in his parish, as she herself learned the importance of service and faith. He set a good example for his children and was known for being generous, caring and kind.

Inside St Nicholas Church where Jane prayed for the first 25 years of her life

Reverend Austen was also a meticulous record keeper, and we can see in the Steventon church registers that he noted every birth, marriage and death.

He would have asked his children to assist him with this chore, and whether Jane was 'helping' her father or having a little fun, we will never know. As the church at Steventon has no vestry, and the key to the door was kept in the hollow of the yew tree, Reverend Austen brought the registers home.

You can read in the Steventon Marriage Register that the

specimen entry has been altered by Jane. This is the page that shows you an example of what to write in each section.

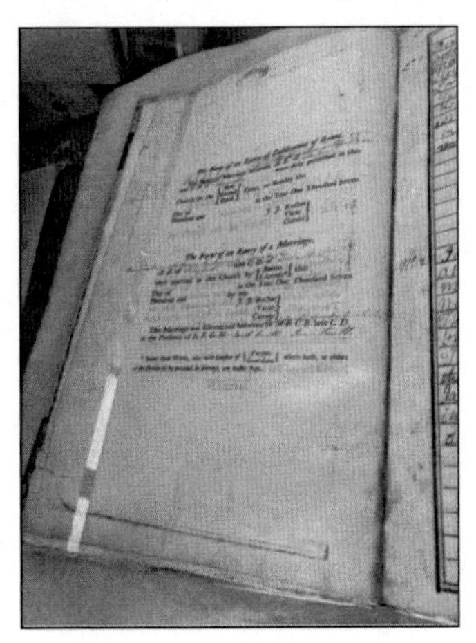

Jane's Scribbles in the Specimen Page of the Steventon Marriage Register

Jane and her siblings were often asked to be witnesses at weddings, and Jane has playfully filled in the form with fictitious names, and then included her own name.

You can read of the marriage between *Henry Frederic Howard Fitzwilliam of London* and *Jane Austen of Steventon*, and also *Edmund Arthur William Mortimer of Liverpool* and *Jane Austen of Steventon.* A witness entry below is between *Jack Smith, Jane Smith*, late *Austen*, in the presence of *Jack Smith, Jane Smith*, and shows Jane's sense of fun.

When free from helping her father with his duties, Jane was known to play the piano, sew, read and write. Her father gave Jane access to his vast library, and purchased her notebooks to encourage her writing.

Jane wrote her first piece of *Juvenilia* when she was 12 years old, initially for her youngest brother Charles, although other pieces are dedicated to family members. Jane would write and Cassandra would draw and paint, and the sheets they used were bound into Volumes and kept for the amusement of the family.

The Austen's were a clever and attractive family, and Jane herself was pretty, described as being tall and slim, with round rosy cheeks, a small mouth, large hazel eyes and brown curly hair.

She was 17 years old when her first two nieces Anne and Fanny were born, and she would go on to become a most treasured aunt. Her niece Caroline said that, '*Her first charm to children was great sweetness of manner. She seemed to love you, and you loved her in return.*'

Her family gave Jane great pleasure and she often prayed for their safety and gave thanks for blessings she received. She went to church every Sunday and was devoted to God.

At 19 years old she received a copy of *A Companion to the Altar: shewing the nature and necessity of a sacramental preparation in order to our worthy receiving the Holy Communion, to which are added prayers and meditations (1793).* It was used as a guide for those about to be confirmed in the Church of England.

Jane's great-niece Florence Austen claimed that '*this book of devotions was always used by Jane*', and it is inscribed with her signature and the date 1794.

It was a happy childhood where Jane's writing flourished. She wrote her first novel *Elinor and Marianne*, now known as *Sense and Sensibility* around 1795. The novel is about the close relationship between two sisters, one with practical good sense and the other sensitive and emotional, who both find love at the end.

Jane's talent was beginning to show, and Jane's father purchased a travel writing slope for her 19th birthday to encourage his daughter to write. She took it with her wherever she went, and kept her novels and quills in its secret compartment.

Jane's niece Marianne shared a charming memory of Jane from when she was young. It was whilst Jane was staying with them at Godmersham in Kent.

Marianne said her aunt Jane would, '*Sit quietly working beside the fire in the library, saying nothing for a good while, and then would suddenly burst out laughing, jump up and run across the room to a table where pens and paper were lying, write something down, and then come back to the fire and go on quietly working as before.*'

This was probably when Jane was writing her most popular novel *First Impressions*, later titled *Pride and Prejudice*. The visits to Kent had opened up a wider pool of wealthier characters for her to draw on, quite different from the Hampshire circle she was used to.

Jane's family enjoyed the novel so much, Mr Austen offered it to the publisher Cadell who later refused it 'sight unseen'.

The days at Steventon Rectory were happy. The family had many friends their own age in the surrounding area, some of whom would stay friends throughout their life. For Jane, there would be trips to Basingstoke for shopping, dancing at balls, walking through the meadows, and visiting friends.

It was here that Jane spent the first 25 years of her life, and where she would write the first drafts of *Sense and Sensibility, Pride and Prejudice* and *Northanger Abbey*.

The great change to Jane's life came with a move to Bath. Mr Austen announced his retirement and that he would pass his living to his eldest son James. It had all been arranged, and in 1801 the Austen family sold their possessions and moved to the city.

This is when Jane's writing stalled and her life became more serious. There were trips to Kent and to London, and holidays to the seaside, and a few chance romances to make these years eventful, though not as happy as the youthful years spent at Steventon.

Bath was a busy place with many visitors. The churches were full, which encouraged chapels to spring up on every corner which required a subscription. This meant that Jane often went to a different church each week, no matter where she was staying, and only the weather would keep her away.

She would often comment on the delivery of sermons which she thought important, and would often mention church in her letters. '*On Sunday we went to Church twice*' and in another letter, *'On leaving Chapel we walked to Lansdowne.'*

It was during these middle years of her life at Bath that Jane's faith was tested.

Anne Lefroy and Jane were friends despite a wide age gap. Jane had greatly admired her and found Anne both interesting and intelligent. As the wife of a clergyman, Anne had taken her duties seriously and taught children in the village and vaccinated many against smallpox.

On 16 December 1804, as Jane celebrated her 29th birthday, the news came that Jane's friend Anne was thrown from a horse and died a few hours later. She was only 55 years old. Jane's brother James conducted the funeral service on 21 December, as she was laid to rest in the churchyard of Holy Trinity & St Andrew.

Four years later, Jane wrote a poem to her memory which begins with the acknowledgement that Anne died on her own birthday. Jane paraphrases Boswell's final tribute to Johnson at the end of her poem, copied from *Johnson's Prayers and Meditations* that she knew well. It was published in 1785 and its passages cited frequently in Boswell's *Life of Johnson*.

To the Memory of Mrs Lefroy who Died Dec:r 16 – My Birthday

The day returns again, my natal day;
What mix'd emotions with the Thought arise!
Beloved friend, four years have pass'd away
Since thou wert snatch'd forever from our eyes.-

The day, commemorative of my birth
Bestowing Life and Light and Hope on me,
Brings back the hour which was thy last on Earth.
Oh! bitter pang of torturing Memory!-

Angelic Woman! past my power to praise
In Language meet, thy Talents, Temper, mind.
Thy solid Worth, they captivating Grace! –
Thou friend and ornament of Humankind! –

At Johnson's death by Hamilton 'twas said,
'Seek we a substitute – Ah! vain the plan,
No second best remains to Johnson dead –
None can remind us even of the Man.'

So we of thee – unequall'd in thy race
Unequall'd thou, as he the first of Men.
Vainly we search around the vacant place,
We ne'er may look upon thy like again.

Come then fond Fancy, thou indulgant Power, –
– Hope is desponding, chill, severe to thee! –
Bless thou, this little portion of an hour,
Let me behold her as she used to be.

I see her here, with all her smiles benign,
Her looks of eager Love, her accents sweet.
That voice and Countenance almost divine! –
Expression, Harmony, alike complete. –

I listen – 'tis not sound alone – 'tis sense,
'Tis Genius, Taste and Tenderness of Soul.
'Tis genuine warmth of heart without pretence
And purity of Mind that crowns the whole.

She speaks; 'tis Eloquence–that grace of Tongue
So rare, so lovely! – Never misapplied
By her to palliate Vice, or deck a Wrong,
She speaks and reasons but on Virtue's side.

Hers is the Energy of Soul sincere.
Her Christian Spirit ignorant to feign,
Seeks but to comfort, heal, enlighten, chear,
Confer a pleasure, or prevent a pain. –

Can ought enhance such Goodness? – Yes, to me,
Her partial favour from my earliest years
Consummates all. – Ah! Give me yet to see
Her smile of Love. – the Vision disappears.

'Tis past and gone–We meet no more below.
Short is the Cheat of Fancy o'er the Tomb.
Oh! might I hope to equal Bliss to go!
To meet thee Angel! in thy future home! –

Fain would I feel an union in they fate,
Fain would I seek to draw an Omen fair
From this connection in our Earthly date.
Indulge the harmless weakness-Reason, spare.-

Jane was to suffer another tragedy a few months later when her father died. She wrote to her brother Frank to break the news, '*Our dear Father has closed his virtuous and happy life, in a death almost as free from suffering as his Children could have wished.*' Jane had loved her father dearly, and must have grieved a great deal.

His death had also brought financial anguish to the Austen ladies, as her father's pension died with him. They now had to rely on their brothers for financial support. After a brief spell in temporary lodgings in Bath, the Austen ladies moved to Southampton to live with Frank and his new wife Mary. They invited Martha Lloyd to move with them as her mother had recently died. As Frank was often away at sea, it was safer and more economical to live together.

The next test of faith came with the sudden death of Edward's wife Elizabeth. She died shortly after giving birth to their eleventh child and the whole family was shocked at the news.

Cassandra was already helping at Godmersham and stayed for months to help care for the young family.

Jane brought Edward's two sons from Winchester School to Southampton to spend time with their aunt. She mentions in a letter that she took them to church to pray for their mother, and how brave they both were.

Jane also felt the loss of her sister-in-law, and would correspond with Fanny, her eldest niece, to give her advice that her mother may have given her.

She also wrote daily to Cassandra, and although Jane's letters do not directly allude to prayers at home, on a Sunday night in 1801 she writes in her letter, '*In the evening we had the Psalms and Lessons, and a sermon at home.*'

Writing out her own prayers saved her carrying the family bible and were easier to read by candlelight.

Jane prayed daily for her family. She writes of God's watchful presence over his children, especially as brothers Frank and Charles were often away at sea, and England was at war with France for most of her life.

> *Guard us and all we love from Evil this night. May the sick and afflicted, be now, and ever thy care; and heartily do we pray for the safety of all that travel by Land or by Sea.*

It was her brother Charles that gave Jane one of her most treasured possessions, her amber topaz cross. He also bought a similar one for Jane's sister Cassandra.

Jane Austen's Topaz Cross

Charles bought the crosses with prize money he received from the Navy for capturing an enemy ship. Jane chided Charles for spending his prize money on a present for her, although she was delighted with the gift.

Jane shared the news with Cassandra in a letter dated 26 May 1801, *'Of what avail is it to take prizes if he lays out the produce in presents to his Sisters. He has been buying Gold chains and Topaz Crosses for us - he must be well scolded.. I shall write again by this post to thank and reproach him. We shall be unbearably fine.'*

The fact that Charles chose crosses for his sisters rather than lockets is significant, alluding to their deep Christian faith.

It was ten years later, when Jane repaid his kindness by writing about William Price giving his sister Fanny a similar cross in *Mansfield Park.* It is said to be Jane's most religious novel and she covers many themes relevant to the church, including a model clergyman in Edmund Bertram, quite different from the comical Mr Collins in *Pride and Prejudice.*

She wrote the novel in its entirety at Chawton Cottage, which the Austen ladies moved into when Jane was 33 years old.

Edward's good fortune had allowed him to give his mother and sisters a cottage to live in for the rest of their days. Jane wrote out how thankful she was in prayer.

We thank thee for with all our hearts for every gracious dispensation, for all the blessings that have attended our lives, for every hour of safety, health and peace, of domestic comfort and innocent enjoyment.

Painting of Chawton Cottage with the Village Pond

At last, there were no more worries about leases, money and the need to constantly move house.

Give us a thankful sense of the Blessings in which we live, of the many comforts of our lot: that we may not deserve to lose them by Discontent or Indifference.

And in giving thanks, Jane would end her day with a prayer to ask God to watch over them and guide her through each day.

Bring us in safety to the beginning of another day and grant that we may rise again with every serious and religious feeling which now directs us.

The move to Chawton Cottage meant that Jane could simply walk to St Nicholas church in the grounds of the Great House. She attended a church service every Sunday, and would walk along the lane past the little cottages, through the meadows to arrive at the pretty church gates.

Jane wrote a charming poem about her fellow church goers in 1807. Sunday was the farm workers only day off, and sometimes the church service could go on for hours. The final verse reads,

Happy the lab'rer in his Sunday cloathes!
In light-drab coat, smart waistcoat, well-darn'd hose,
And hat upon his head, to church he goes;
As oft, with conscious pride, he downward throws
A glance upon the ample cabbage rose
Which, stuck in button-hole, regales his nose,
He envies not the gayest London beaux.
In church he takes his seat among the rows,
Pays to the place the reverence he owes,
Likes best the prayers whose meaning least he knows,
Lists to the sermon in a softening doze,
And rouses joyous at the welcome close.

It seems Jane was happy once again, back in a little village in Hampshire, and her writing flourished.

Jane Austen's Writing Desk at Chawton Cottage

It was here at Chawton that Jane would rewrite her earlier novels, *Sense and Sensibility*, *Pride and Prejudice* and *Northanger Abbey*, and write *Mansfield Park*, *Emma* and *Persuasion* in their entirety.

Mrs Austen's footman, William Littleworth, recalled how he often saw Jane writing at the little table through the cottage window.

Jane counted her blessings, and although she does not write too deeply about religion in her novels, she does include church matters and a variety of clergymen. Her grandfather, father, two brothers, cousins, and other relations were all clergymen, and she probably saw their faults as well as their strengths.

Jane has the unique ability to make her readers judge her characters by their actions and what they say.

She gives us three wonderful clergymen in Edmund Bertram, Henry Tilney and Edward Ferrars. Mr Elton of *Emma* is another decent clergyman who enjoys the many social aspects of his role, although most of Jane's followers like (and dislike) Mr Collins for his characterful personality.

As for Jane's heroines, they all endure a journey of self-discovery. Elizabeth Bennet is forced to admit, '*I have courted prepossession and ignorance, and driven reason away, where either were concerned. Till this moment I never knew myself.*'

Emma undergoes a similar self-revelation and prompted by her friend Mr Knightley, has to say sorry for her treatment of Miss Bates the next day.

Marianne Dashwood says '*I wonder at my recovery, -wonder that the very eagerness of my desire to live, to have time for atonement to my God, and to you all, did not kill me at once… Whenever I looked toward the past, I saw some duty neglected, or some failing indulged.*'

As for Mr Darcy in *Pride and Prejudice,* he is so much more attractive to the ladies when he is seen at church twice in one week. She writes '*Mr Darcy they had seen only at church.*'

Pride and Prejudice *written by the 'Author of* Sense and Sensibility'

As for the word 'God', Jane writes it as an exclamation only in the most serious of moments.

Mr Darcy is compelled to exclaim at seeing Elizabeth's distress at Lydia's elopement, '*Good God! What is the matter?*' Marianne is cut by Willoughby, '*Good God! Willoughby what is the meaning of this?*' Captain Wentworth after Louisa's fall from the

Cobb exclaims, '*Oh God! her father and mother*', and a final '*Good God!*' falls from his lips when he learns that Anne will accept his hand in marriage.

Jane often commented that sermons should be delivered in an animated fashion, and good delivery was important.

In a letter to her nephew Edward on 16 December 1816, her birthday, she writes, '*Uncle Henry writes very superior Sermons*' and adds mischievously, '*You & I must try to get hold of one or two, & put them into our Novels; -it would be a fine help to a volume; & we could make our Heroine read it aloud of a Sunday Evening.*'

She could have been thinking of her novel *Mansfield Park*, published a couple of years earlier, where Fanny Price refers to prayers at Sotherton. '*A whole family assembling regularly for the purpose of prayer, is fine.*'

As Jane was writing *Mansfield Park* her cousin Eliza died. Eliza had been a central figure in Jane's life from when she was a young girl. She was known affectionately as Betsy, and was pretty, full of life and so much fun.

Maybe Jane remembered their happy childhood and the theatricals in the barn at Steventon when she wrote similar scenes into *Mansfield Park*. Some speculate that Eliza inspired the character Mary Crawford, who was very charming and enjoyed city life and sociability. Eliza later married Jane's brother Henry, and Jane nursed her through a long illness. She died in London four years before Jane.

Jane herself had started to feel unwell in 1816 from what we now know was Addison's disease, for which there was no cure.

For a short time, Jane's condition improved and in the New Year she started a new novel she called *The Brothers*, later retitled *Sanditon*.

In a letter dated early March 1817, Jane felt better and wrote to her niece Caroline about her '*fine flow of literary ardour*' prompted by a receipt of nearly twenty pounds from Egerton for sales from the Second Edition of *Sense and Sensibility*.

However, this improvement was short lived, and on 18 March,

mid chapter, Jane stopped writing *Sanditon* and laid down her quill for the last time.

Her family was so concerned about the deterioration in her health, they took her to Winchester to consult a surgeon at the new Winchester Hospital. Dr Lyford was an excellent doctor and an old family friend, and tended to Jane through her final months of illness.

College Street, Winchester in 1838

Jane stayed with Cassandra at 8 College Street in rooms on the first floor with the little bow window. The lease was arranged by Elizabeth Bigg, a childhood friend, who visited Jane every day.

Jane's family also visited often, and in May 1817, Jane wrote a letter about their kindness, '*I can only cry over it, and pray to God to bless them more and more.*'

Jane had kept her faith and Christian beliefs throughout her life, and a little time before her death she received the Holy Communion from her brothers James and Henry, '*Before excessive bodily weakness might have rendered her perception unequal to her wishes.*'

At dawn on 18 July 1817, Jane died peacefully in the arms of her loving sister Cassandra. She was the first of the siblings to die at just 41 years of age, and it was a devastating blow to her family.

Cassandra writes to their niece Fanny of Jane's last hours.

> *I have lost a treasure, such a Sister, such a friend as never can have been surpassed, -She was the sun of my life, the gilder of every pleasure, the soother of every sorrow, I had not a thought concealed from her, & it is as if I had lost a part of myself. When I asked her if there was any thing she wanted, her answer was she wanted nothing but death & some of her words were 'God grant me patience, Pray for me, oh Pray for me.*

Jane's funeral took place on 24 July and she is buried in the north aisle of Winchester Cathedral. Her family wrote her epitaph together, and there is no mention of her writing, just the great loss felt by her family.

THE BENEVOLENCE OF HER HEART,
THE SWEETNESS OF HER TEMPER AND
THE EXTRAORDINARY ENDOWMENTS OF HER MIND
OBTAINED THE REGARD OF ALL WHO KNEW HER AND
THE WARMEST LOVE OF HER INTIMATE CONNECTIONS.
THEIR GRIEF IS IN PROPORTION TO THEIR AFFECTION
THEY KNOW THEIR LOSS TO BE IRREPARABLE
BUT IN THEIR DEEPEST AFFLICTION THEY ARE CONSOLED
BY A FIRM THOUGH HUMBLE HOPE THAT HER CHARITY
DEVOTION, FAITH AND PURITY HAVE RENDERED
HER SOUL ACCEPTABLE IN THE SIGHT OF HER
REDEEMER.

It seems fitting that the final sentence talks of her charity, devotion, faith and purity.

Jane Austen's Gravestone laid into the floor of Winchester Cathedral

Jane was always fondly remembered by her family, and they wrote memories of their childhood with 'Aunt Jane'.

Jane's niece Caroline, the daughter of her eldest brother James, wrote a loving passage about her aunt Jane in her own *Memoirs*.

> *I need scarcely say she was dearly loved by her family. Her Brothers were very proud of her - Her literary fame, at the close of her life, was only just spreading - but they were proud of her talents, which they even then estimated highly - proud of her home virtues, of her cheerful spirit - of her pleasant looks - and each loved afterwards to fancy a resemblance in some daughter of his own, to the dear "Aunt Jane", whose perfect equal they yet never expected to see.*

Jane's niece Mary Jane that the family said looked like Jane at the same age, with baby George, the children of Jane's brother Francis

JANE AUSTEN'S PRAYERS

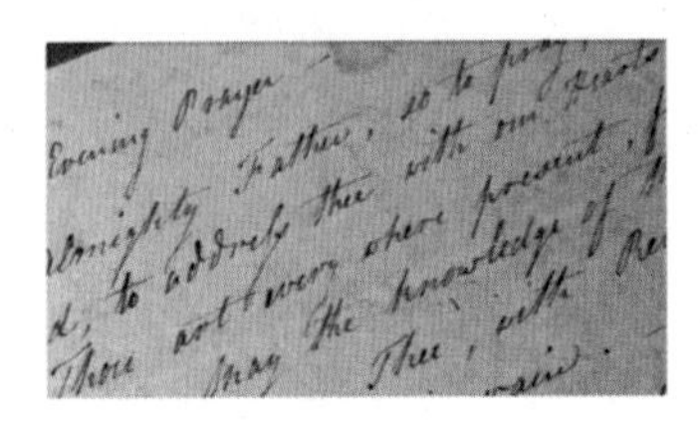

Jane's three surviving prayers are shown on the following pages. The image of each prayer is followed with the transcript for easy reading.

The prayers are in their original order, with the Lord's Prayer added at the end of each one as Jane intended.

This book makes Jane's prayers accessible to everyone. To read them and to pray along with Jane is to enter into her heart and experience the spirituality of one of the world's most beloved writers.

Prayers Composed
by my ever dear
Sister Jane

PART I
EVENING PRAYER

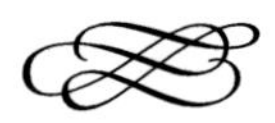

Give us grace, Almighty Father, so to pray, as to deserve to be heard, to address Thee with our Hearts, as with our lips.

Thou art every where present, from Thee no secret can be hid; may the knowledge of this, teach us to fix our Thoughts on Thee, with Reverence and Devotion that we pray not in vain.

Look with Mercy on the Sins we have this day committed, and in Mercy make us feel them deeply, that our Repentance may be sincere, and our Resolutions stedfast of endeavouring against the commission of such in future.

Teach us to understand the sinfulness of our own Hearts, and bring to our knowledge every fault of Temper and every evil Habit in which we have indulged to the discomfort of our fellow-creatures, and the danger of our own Souls.

May we now, and on each return of night, consider how the past day has been spent by us, what have been our prevailing Thoughts, Words, and Actions during it, and how far we can acquit ourselves of Evil.

Evening Prayer –

Give us grace, Almighty Father, so to pray, as to deserve to be heard, to address thee with our Hearts, as with our Lips. Thou art every where present, from Thee no secret can be hid; May the knowledge of this, teach us to fix our Thoughts on Thee, with Reverence & Devotion that we pray not in vain. –

Look with Mercy on the Sins we have this day committed, & in Mercy make us feel them deeply, that our Repentance may be sincere, and our Resolutions stedfast of endeavouring against the commission of such in future. – Teach us to understand the sinfulness of our own Hearts, and bring to our knowledge every fault of Temper and every evil Habit in which we may have indulged to the discomfort of our fellow-creatures, and the danger of our own Souls. – May we now, and on each return of Night, consider how the past day has been spent by us, what have been our prevailing Thoughts, Words and Actions during it, and how far we can acquit ourselves of Evil.

Have we thought irreverently of Thee, have we disobeyed thy commandments, have we neglected any known duty, or willingly given pain to any human being? Incline us to ask our Hearts these questions Oh! God, and save us from deceiving ourselves by Pride or Vanity.

Give us a thankful sense of the Blessings in which we live, of the many comforts of our lot: that we may not deserve to lose them by Discontent or Indifference.

Be gracious to our Necessities, and guard us, and all we love, from Evil this night. May the sick and afflicted, be now, and ever thy care; and heartily do we pray for the safety of all that travel by Land or by Sea, for the comfort and protection of the Orphan and Widow and that thy pity may be shown, upon all Captives and Prisoners.

Above all other blessings Oh! God, for ourselves, and our fellow-creatures, we implore Thee to quicken our sense of thy Mercy in the redemption of the World, of the Value of that Holy Religion in which we have been brought up, that we may not, by..

Have we thought irreverently of Thee, have we disobeyed thy Commandments, have we neglected any known Duty, or willingly given pain to any Human Being? — Incline us to ask our Hearts these questions Oh! God, and save us from de=ceiving ourselves by Pride or Vanity.

Give us a thankful sense of the Blessings in which we live, of the many comforts of our Lot; that we may not deserve to lose them by Discontent or Indifference.

Be Gracious to our Necessities, and guard us, and all we love, from Evil this night. May the sick and afflicted, be now, & ever thy care; and heartily do we pray for the safety of all that tra=vel by Land or by Sea, for the comfort & protection of the Orphan & Widow, & that thy pity may be shewn, upon all Captives & Prisoners.

Above all other blessings Oh! God, for ourselves, & our fellow-creatures, we implore Thee to quicken our sense of thy Mercy in the redemption of the world, of the Value of that Holy Religion in which we have been brought up, that we may not, by our own neglect, throw away the Salvation Thou hast given us, nor be Christians only in name. Hear us Almighty God, for His sake who has redeemed us, and taught us thus to pray.

Our Father which art in Heaven,
Hallowed be Thy name.
Thy kingdom come.
Thy will be done in earth, as it is in heaven.
Give us this day our daily bread.
And forgive us our debts, as we forgive our debtors.
And lead us not into temptation, but deliver us from evil:
For Thine is the kingdom, and the power, and the glory, for ever.
Amen.

our own neglect, throw away the Salvation Thou hast given us, nor be Christians only in name. — Hear us Almighty God, for His sake who has redeemed us, & taught us thus to pray. —

Our Father which art in Heaven &c

PART II
FATHER OF HEAVEN

Father of Heaven! Whose goodness has brought us in safety to the close of this day, dispose our hearts in fervent prayer.

Another day is now gone, and added to those, for which we were before accountable. Teach us Almighty Father, to consider this solemn truth, as we should do, that we may feel the importance of every day, and every hour as it passes, and earnestly strive to make a better use of what Thy goodness may yet bestow on us, than we have done of the time past.

Give us grace to endeavour after a truly Christian spirit to seek to attain that temper of Forbearance and Patience, of which our Blessed Saviour has set us the highest example; and which, while it prepares us for the spiritual happiness of the life to come, will secure to us the best enjoyment of what this world can give.

Incline us Oh God! to think humbly of ourselves, to be severe only in the examination of our own conduct, to consider our fellow creatures with kindness, and to judge of all they say and do with that charity which we would desire from them ourselves.

Father of Heaven! whose goodness has brought us in safety to the close of this day, dispose our Hearts in fervent prayer.

Another day is now gone, & added to those, for which we were before accountable. Teach us Almighty Father, to consider this solemn Truth, as we should do, that we may feel the importance of every day, & every hour as it passes, & earnestly strive to make a better use of what Thy Goodness may yet bestow on us, than we have done of the Time past.

Give us Grace to endeavour after a truly christian Spirit to seek to attain that temper of Forbearance & Patience, of which our Blessed Saviour has set us the highest Example, and which while it prepares us for the spiritual Happiness of the life to come, will secure to us the best enjoyment of what this World can give. Incline us Oh God! to think humbly of ourselves, to be severe only in the examination of our own conduct, to consider our fellow creatures with kindness, & to judge of all they say & do with that Charity which we would desire from them ourselves.

We thank thee with all our hearts for every gracious dispensation, for all the Blessings that have attended our lives, for every hour of safety, health and peace, of domestic comfort and innocent enjoyment. We feel that we have been blessed far beyond any thing that we have deserved; and though we cannot but pray for a continuance of all these mercies, we acknowledge our unworthiness of them and implore thee to pardon the presumption of our desires.

Keep us Oh! Heavenly Father from Evil this night. Bring us in safely to the beginning of another day and grant that we may rise again with every serious and religious feeling which now directs us.

May thy mercy be extended over all mankind, bringing the ignorant to the knowledge of thy truth, awakening the impenitent, touching the hardened. Look with compassion upon the afflicted of every condition, assuage the pangs of disease, comfort the broken in spirit.

We thank thee with all our hearts for every gracious dispen:sation, for all the Blessings that have attended our Lives, for every hour of safety, health & peace, of domestic comfort & inno:cent enjoyment. We feel that we have been blessed far beyond any thing that we have deserved; and though we cannot but pray for a continuance of all these Mercies, we acknowledge our unworthiness of them & implore Thee to pardon the presumption of our desires.

Keep us oh! Heavenly Father from Evil this night. — Bring us in safety to the beginning of another day & grant that we may rise again with every serious & religious feeling which now directs us.

May thy mercy be extended over all Mankind, bringing the Ignorant to the knowledge of thy Truth, awakening the Im:penitent, touching the Hardened. — Look with compassion upon the afflicted of every condition, assuage the pangs of disease, comfort the broken in spirit.

More particularly do we pray for the safety and welfare of our own family & friends wheresoever dispersed, be:seeching Thee to avert from them all material & lasting Evil of Body or Mind; & may we by the assistance of thy Holy Spirit so conduct ourselves on Earth as to secure an Eternity of Happiness with each other in thy Heavenly Kingdom. Grant this most merciful Father, for the sake of our Blessed Sa:viour in whose Holy Name & Words we further address Thee.

Our Father &c

More particularly do we pray for the safety and welfare of our own family and friends wheresoever dispersed, beseeching Thee to avert from them all material and lasting evil of body or mind; and may we by the assistance of thy Holy Spirit so conduct ourselves on earth as to secure an eternity of happiness with each other in thy heavenly kingdom. Grant this most merciful Father, for the sake of our blessed saviour in whose holy name and words we further address thee.

Our Father which art in Heaven,
Hallowed be Thy name.
Thy kingdom come.
Thy will be done in earth, as it is in heaven.
Give us this day our daily bread.
And forgive us our debts, as we forgive our debtors.
And lead us not into temptation, but deliver us from evil:
For Thine is the kingdom, and the power, and the glory, for ever.
Amen.

We thank thee with all our hearts for every gracious dispen:
:sation, for all the Blessings that have attended our Lives, for
every hour of safety, health & peace, of domestic comfort & inno:
:cent enjoyment. We feel that we have been blessed far beyond
any thing that we have deserved; and though we cannot but
pray for a continuance of all these Mercies, we acknowledge our
unworthiness of them & implore Thee to pardon the presumption
of our desires.

Keep us oh! Heavenly Father from Evil this night. —
Bring us in safety to the beginning of another day & grant
that we may rise again with every serious & religious feeling
which now directs us.

May thy mercy be extended over all Mankind, bringing
the Ignorant to the knowledge of thy Truth, awakening the Im:
penitent, touching the Hardened. — Look with compassion upon
the afflicted of every condition, assuage the pangs of disease,
comfort the broken in spirit.

More particularly do we pray for the safety and
welfare of our own family & friends wheresoever dispersed, be:
:seeching Thee to avert from them all material & lasting Evil
of Body or Mind; & may we by the assistance of thy Holy
Spirit so conduct ourselves on Earth as to secure an Eternity
of Happiness with each other in thy Heavenly Kingdom. Grant
this most merciful Father, for the sake of our Blessed Sa:
:viour in whose Holy Name & words we further address Thee.

Our Father &c

PART III
ALMIGHTY GOD

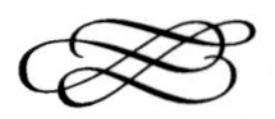

Almighty God! Look down with mercy on Thy servants here assembled and accept the petitions now offered up unto Thee.

Pardon Oh! God the offences of the past day. We are conscious of many frailties; we remember with shame and contrition, many evil thoughts and neglected duties; and we have perhaps sinned against Thee and against our fellow-creatures in many instances of which we have no remembrance. Pardon Oh God! whatever thou has seen amiss in us, and give us a stronger desire of resisting every evil inclination and weakening every habit of sin. Thou knowest the infirmity of our nature, and the temptations which surround us. Be Thou merciful, oh Heavenly Father! to creatures so formed and situated.

We bless Thee for every comfort of our past and present existence, for our health of body and of mind and for every other source of happiness which Thou hast bountifully bestowed on us and with which we close this day, imploring their continuance from Thy Fatherly goodness, with a more grateful sense of them, than they have hitherto excited. May the comforts of every day, be thankfully felt by us, may they prompt a willing obedience of thy commandments and a benevolent spirit toward every fellow-creature.

Have mercy Oh..

Almighty God! Look down with mercy on thy Servants here assembled & accept the petitions now offer'd up unto thee.

Pardon Oh God! the offences of the past day. We are conscious of many frailties; we remember with shame & contrition, many evil Thoughts & neglected duties, & we have perhaps sinned against Thee & against our fellow-creatures in many instances of which we have now no remembrance. — Pardon Oh God! whatever thou hast seen amiss in us, & give us a stronger desire of resisting every evil inclination & weakening every habit of sin. Thou knowest the infirmity of our nature, & the temptations which surround us. Be thou merciful, Oh Heavenly Father! to Creatures so formed & situated.

We bless thee for every comfort of our past and present existence, for our health of Body & of mind & for every other source of happiness which Thou hast bountifully bestowed on us & with which we close this day, imploring their continuance from thy Fatherly goodness, with a more grateful sense of them, than they have hitherto excited. May the comforts of every day, be thankfully felt by us, may they prompt a willing obedience of thy commandments & a benevolent spirit towards every fellow-creature.

Have mercy Oh

Gracious Father! upon all that are now suffering from whatsoever cause, that are in any circumstance of danger or distress. Give them patience under every affliction, strengthen, comfort and relieve them.

To Thy goodness we commend ourselves this night beseeching Thy protection of us through its darkness and dangers. We are helpless and dependent; graciously preserve us. For all whom we love and value, for every friend and connection, we equally pray; however divided and far asunder, we know that we are alike before Thee, and under Thine eye. May we be equally united in Thy faith and fear, in fervent devotion towards Thee, and in Thy merciful protection this night.

Pardon Oh Lord! the imperfections of these our prayers, and accept them through the mediation of our Blessed Saviour, in whose Holy words, we further address Thee.

Our Father which art in Heaven,
Hallowed be Thy name.
Thy kingdom come.
Thy will be done in earth, as it is in heaven.
Give us this day our daily bread.
And forgive us our debts, as we forgive our debtors.
And lead us not into temptation, but deliver us from evil:
For Thine is the kingdom, and the power, and the glory, for ever.
Amen.

gracious Father! upon all that are now suffering
from whatsoever cause, that are in any circumstance
of danger or distress — give them patience under
every affliction, strengthen, comfort & relieve them.
To Thy goodness we commend ourselves this night
beseeching thy protection of us through its dark=
=ness & dangers. We are helpless & dependant;
graciously preserve us — For all whom we love
& value, for every Friend & connection, we equally
pray; However divided & far asunder, we know that
we are alike before Thee, & under thine Eye. May
we be equally united in Thy Faith & Fear, in
fervent devotion towards Thee, & in Thy merciful
Protection this night. Pardon Oh Lord! the im=
=perfections of these our Prayers, & accept them
through the mediation of our Blessed Saviour, in
whose Holy words, we farther address thee; Our Father

CLOSING PRAYER

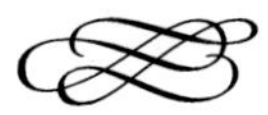

Another day is now gone, and added to those,
for which we were before accountable.
Teach us almighty father, to consider this solemn truth,
as we should do, that we may feel the importance of every day,
and every hour as it passes,
and earnestly strive to make a better use
of what thy goodness may yet bestow on us,
than we have done of the time past.

— JANE AUSTEN

BIBLIOGRAPHY

Jane Austen's novels, letters and minor works are cited using her first name to avoid confusion with the many other Austen family members.

Jane Austen's Letters, collected and edited by Deirdre Le Faye, and published by Oxford University Press in 1995, is the source for excerpts of Jane's correspondence. This edition preserves Jane's spelling and punctuation, and respects her use of dashes, commas and exclamation marks.

Jane Austen's novels are in the public domain, although I often read my own library of special editions.

My research is ongoing, and I have referenced many books, both old and new, family papers and letters, novels and books about Jane Austen.
There are too many to mention, though I have listed the key sources of research below:

Austen, Caroline. *My Aunt Jane: A Memoir.* Sarsen Press, 1867.
Austen Leigh, J. E. *A Memoir of Jane Austen by Her Nephew*. London, 1871.
Austen Leigh, William and Richard Arthur. *Jane Austen Her Life and Letters, A Family Record.* Smith, Elder & Co, 1913.
Blythe, Ronald. *A Country Parson, James Woodforde's Diary 1759-1802*. Nicholas, 1985.
Byrne, Paula. *The Real Jane Austen.* Harperpress, 2013.
Chapman, R. W. *Jane Austen Selected Letters*. London, 1954.
Chapman, R. W. *Minor Works of Jane Austen*. London, 1954.
Collins, Irene. *Jane Austen: The Parson's Daughter.* Hambledon Press, 1998.
Gilson, David. *A Biography of Jane Austen*. London, 1986.
Hill, Constance. *Jane Austen: Her Homes & Her Friends.* 1901.
Jenkins, Elizabeth. *Jane Austen: A Biography*. Sphere, 1972.
Keynes, Geoffrey. *Jane Austen: A Bibliography*. Franklin, 1968.
Lane, Maggie. *Jane Austen's England*. London, 1986.
Lefroy, Helen. *Jane Austen.* The History Press, 1997.
Le Faye, Deirdre. *Jane Austen: A Family Record.* Oxford University Press, 1989.
Leigh, William Austen and Austen Leigh, Richard Arthur. London, 1913.
Stovel, Bruce. *A Nation Improving in Religion: Jane Austen's Prayers and Their Place in Her Life and Art*. London, 1994.

I would like to thank the following for giving me their support and time in researching and writing about Jane Austen:

Alton Library (Jane Austen Collection), Bath Records Office, Chawton House, F. W. Olin Library, Hampshire Cultural Trust, Hampshire Records Office, Jane Austen House Museum, Winchester Cathedral, Winchester College.

I would also like to mention the passing of Deirdre Le Faye. For many people who study Jane Austen, she was the leading biographer and scholar who researched Jane's life and times for over forty years. Deirdre published many books about Jane and wrote the ultimate 'bible', *Jane Austen: A Family Record,* amongst others. She had an extraordinary character, was passionate and patient, and whenever she came to visit Chawton there was always a stir of excitement in the air. She will be remembered dearly.

LIST OF ILLUSTRATIONS

ACKNOWLEDGEMENTS

Like many people, I read Jane Austen's novels in my teenage years and enjoyed reading about the many romances, balls, family squabbles, misunderstandings, passions, and of course the happy endings.

I am fortunate to live near Jane Austen's Chawton Cottage, and have spent many hours in the village, walking through the lanes and over the fields, and praying in the church, just as Jane did over 200 years ago. The more time I spend with Jane, the more I enjoy her.

I started researching Jane's life and novels many years ago after a volunteering project, and I have been lucky enough to see the many treasures relating to Jane's life and those of her family. I want to thank the many helpful people who have been patient and generous with their time. This includes all the staff and volunteers who work at the many museums, libraries, offices, and churches I have visited. It always makes me smile that everyone seems to refer to me as 'the lady writing the Jane books', and everyone knows who Jane is!

I would also like to thank the many other Jane Austen followers around the world. I enjoy reading your books, blogs, emails, and social media posts that drop into my email. Hopefully we will see each other at those wonderful Jane Austen events where we can talk about Jane for hours on end. This book is for you in thanks for the friendship, encouragement and support you have given me for so many years.

Thinking of my family and friends, I am also grateful. My family is similar to Jane's in that we are all close, at least in our hearts if not in distance. To my friends around the world, both old and new, who have supported me and my writing along with my various expeditions, I thank you.

I feel humbled to have been given this opportunity to share Jane's original prayer sheets with you. I have read them most evenings since I set eyes on them, and hope they will give you as much comfort as they gave Jane all those years ago.

Please remember that you are not alone. We are praying with you and for you, and that God watches over us and blesses us all.

SUPPORTING CHAWTON HOUSE

Thank you for buying *Jane Austen's Prayers*. A portion of the royalties from this prayer book will go directly to Chawton House. Jane fondly called it the 'Great House' and often walked along the lane to visit her brother Edward and his family, and often mentions it in her letters.

Edward had eleven children and he often stayed at Chawton House with his family whilst visiting his Hampshire relations. He inherited the estate from his adoptive parents, which has St Nicholas church in its grounds, and where Jane worshipped whilst living at Chawton Cottage.

Today, Chawton House is an internationally-renowned research institution, working in partnership with scholars and universities across the globe. With a focus on early women writers, they have a unique collection of women's writing to encourage and inspire future generations.

For Jane Austen followers, there is an extensive library of first edition novels that are written by Jane, and books read by Jane and her family. You can see Anne Sharp's copy of *Emma*, one of only a few bound copies that Jane was given as the author, and signed music books with Jane's music notes scribbled on them.

Read more about their work at https://chawtonhouse.org.

ABOUT THE AUTHOR

Emma Darlington wanted to be an explorer and live her life at sea, until she discovered that dusty old books, churches, and museums are generally found on land. She is passionate about Jane Austen, the Regency period, carriages, and corsets, and has written five non-fiction books on the subject including *Jane Austen's Prayers*, the first time Jane's handwritten prayers have appeared in print.

Emma loves to travel and is usually away on an adventure researching her next travel guide or mystery novel. A digital nomad, Emma works in international communications and supports a number of charities.

On dry land, she spends a lot of time drinking tea in Jane Austen's village of Chawton, England.

ALSO BY EMMA DARLINGTON

JANE AUSTEN 200: CELEBRATING HER LIFE 200 YEARS AFTER HER DEATH

Who was the mysterious Jane Austen? A quiet country girl who was fond of retail and romance and dancing ? Or a strong-minded woman who knew about war, empire and business, who chose to remain unmarried, write novels, and settle for nothing less than her own Mr Darcy?

Jane Austen 200 is filled with unseen photographs and accompanying commentary that illuminate Jane's life to take you on a journey 200 years after her death.

ISBN Print: 978-1-8382-8112-0

ISBN eBook: 978-1-8382-8113-7

JANE AUSTEN TRAVEL GUIDE

Follow in Jane's footsteps to see where she lived, danced, shopped, visited her friends and family, worshipped, and of course - wrote her novels!

This book is filled with detailed maps and walks through Jane's villages, plus original photographs of her treasures, quotes from her novels and letters, and written commentary for your visit to Jane Austen's England. Or simply follow in Jane Austen's footsteps from the comfort of your own armchair.

Filled with travel advice and quick tips to take you on your own Jane Austen journey.

ISBN Print: 978-1-8382-8115-1

ISBN eBook: 978-1-8382-8114-4

Made in United States
Orlando, FL
01 October 2024